Romany Legends Daniel and Dolly Buckley, The Gypsy Way

Romany Legends Daniel and Dolly Buckley, The Gypsy Way

Mary King

Matador
9 Priory Business Park,
Wistow Road, Kibworth Beauchamp,
Leicestershire. LE8 0RX
Tel: 0116 279 2299
Email: books@troubador.co.uk
Web: www.troubador.co.uk/matador
Twitter: @matadorbooks

ISBN 978 1788032 612

British Library Cataloguing in Publication Data.
A catalogue record for this book is available from the British Library.

Printed and bound by CPI Group (UK) Ltd, Croydon, CR0 4YY
Typeset in 11pt Aldine401 BT by Troubador Publishing Ltd, Leicester, UK

Matador is an imprint of Troubador Publishing Ltd

*I dedicate this book to my beloved mother and father, Dolly and Daniel Buckley.
I would like to thank my daughter Marisa for her help in writing this book, and
thank you to Jo Roberts for all her help and patience.*

Prologue

This book has been a long time coming. Over the years many of my family and friends have asked me about my gypsy life, and what it was like to grow up as a true Romany gypsy. I've shared some anecdotes with them and talked about my past, but every time I do, I realise that there is just so much more to tell.

Many of the gypsies of today will be amazed by my upbringing, as it won't be the familiar gypsy way that they live and breathe now; but it was the only way of life I knew as a child, and it was the same for my father who made sure that I understood and respected the gypsy traditions.

My father was a fascinating man, who could spend hours telling stories about his life. He was a kind man, and a fair man, and he was held in high regard by everyone that met him. So much so that many children were named after him in recognition of the respect he had earned in the traveller community and beyond. My mother was also a kind soul, with a great sense of humour that endeared her to people straight away. She was a petite woman but with a personality and determination so large that it more than made up for her small stature.

Together my parents had an extremely happy existence, and I feel blessed that I was born into their family. They faced many struggles on a daily basis but they still battled through with a determination that is rarely seen today.

Up until now I haven't had the time to sit down and put pen to paper, but now, with my children all grown up, and my daily life finally becoming slightly less hectic, it seems right that I take the time to tell my story properly, to share with you the true, Romany gypsy way of life.

By writing this book I would like future generations to understand and appreciate how different their lives are today to the lives of those before them. The changes in attitudes and lifestyles between the generations are quite remarkable, and I hope that by telling my story I can inspire others to hold on to the true gypsy traditions.

As time has passed, it saddens me that these traditions are becoming lost in modern society, and I feel I have a duty and a will to share those traditions in these pages, so that the forgotten gypsy ways can be recorded in history.

Chapter 1

Where it all Began

So, I suppose I should begin by telling you a bit about myself. I'm Mary Rose King, a sixty-three-year-old woman living comfortably in rural Essex with my husband Eddie. We have been happily married for forty-four blissful years, and in that time we have raised three wonderful children: Josie, Karl and Marisa. All three of our children have now married and started their own families, meaning that Eddie and I now have six beautiful grandchildren to dote on: Antoinette, Josephine, James, Karl, Mary-Rose and Tommy.

I myself am one of five children, with my sister, Lilly, and my brothers Mark, John and Richard. They too live nearby with their families and grandchildren, increasing our family numbers to monumental figures.

I've started this book by talking about my family because 'family' and everything that word stands for is extremely important to me. Family represents my heritage, my support network and the people who are loved and give love unconditionally. This is why I feel so blessed to have so many of my relatives living so nearby; it is truly magnificent, and the close bond that we all share fills me with pride.

I have dedicated my life to raising my family and to keeping a nice home, meaning I am always busy; either helping with my grandchildren, working to keep our home clean and tidy, or making sure that the gardens and outside spaces are well kept. I feel extremely grateful that I have such a nice home and lifestyle, but it does also remind me just how different my life is today to how it was growing up as a child.

I was a child in the 1950s and back then things were very different, not least because there wasn't the same kind of healthcare support that we have now, particularly when it comes to having a baby. A local midwife helped to deliver me, and my mother was considered fortunate to have that help. I was born in the wagon that my parents lived in, and that I subsequently lived in for many years. By all accounts my sister was a Godsend when I was born, even though she was only eleven years old, she took up the roles that my mother had to forego to look after me.

My brothers, sisters and I had a tough life; as a gypsy child in the 1950s nothing was easy. We had none of the modern day luxuries that we all take for granted, and electricity was certainly a thing of fantasy in our wagon. Look around you now; look at the appliances and devices you have in your home, at your disposal to make your life easier. I had none of those things; no electric kettle, no washing machine, no dishwasher, no electric iron, no vacuum cleaner. The things we all have in our homes today were things that I and my parents could only dream of back then. Not only did we not have electricity but we also didn't have gas, clear running water or cars. The simplest of tasks like preparing a meal or having a bath became laborious missions that would test even the strongest mind. We managed though; we always had a fire on the go with a kettle hanging over it boiling water, and my sister was always on hand to help cook meals outside on the fire, wash clothes in a tub over the fire, and to walk with my father to the shop to gather food supplies. She did what she could to help my mother, particularly when I was a young baby, and any of us now would do the same for our own families.

Life was tough in the early days and in stark comparison to the way we live today, but the early days were where it all began, namely with my father… Daniel Buckley.

Daniel

Daniel was the much loved son of John and Lucy Buckley; he was born in the coastal town of Southend in Essex, in a place called Lucy's Wood, which was actually named after his mother Lucy as this is where she spent so much of her time.

John and Lucy Buckley were the loving parents to nine children all together, with a split of five girls; Affy, Councey, Sissy, Linda and Clara, and four boys; Rodney, Mark, John and of course my father, Daniel. With so many children, at times space in the wagon became a bit of an issue, but thankfully, as with most gypsy children, a lot of their young lives were spent outside either working or playing. John and Lucy Buckley slept in the main wagon with the younger children, and those old enough to have that little bit of freedom slept in the cart close by. It worked for them, and in the evenings they would build a fire outside the wagon and sit around as a family cooking, talking about their days, and keeping warm as best they could, which was sometimes difficult, especially in the winter months. It was those bitter months that made living in such close confinement a Godsend, as there's no better way to keep warm than snuggling up close to your brothers and sisters.

As a child during the second world war, Daniel Buckley lived in a time where men and women were called to serve their country, and whole families pulled together in order to serve one another. It was a time when rationing impacted on everyday life, and men were often away from their family homes for some time, leaving women and children to survive without them. Having spoken to him about this time there is one vivid memory that has stayed with him since he was just three years old. He told me that he and his mother were working in a pea field, picking peas with a large group of travellers. It was a job he enjoyed as while the others worked furiously to pick the produce he spent most of his time sampling the produce, with his mother turning a blind eye to his cheeky ways. It was while he was happily picking peas that the roar of a plane rumbled in the distance. Everyone in the field that day ceased their picking and looked up to the sky. He remembers an eerie silence before the panic kicked in. He was too young to really understand what was happening but overhead a German fighter plane was charging towards them. Daniel's mother, my grandmother, had no intention of waiting to see what the German plane had in store for them, and she quickly swept Daniel up in her arms and ran into a ditch at the side of the field. Her motherly instincts kicked in and she swamped him with her body as the plane roared above them. There were no bombs dropped that day, but Daniel never forgot the feeling of dread that engulfed that pea field, or the noise of the enemy above.

Thankfully the war passed him by without much more disturbance and his childhood continued rather uneventfully. He didn't ever go to school though as reading and writing just weren't a priority for him. He knew what he wanted to do with his life, and what his job was... he had to help his family to make money and lead a good life. And he knew he could do that with hard graft and a good attitude to work, something which he had in bucket loads.

The family picking peas

It was when he was nine years old that his father, John Buckley, sent him off on his first mission to sell a horse. The buyer lived right on the other side of Southend, making the journey a long and arduous one, but that didn't faze him; my father was a hard worker even from that young age and he would do whatever it took to earn a living. He rose early the next morning and packed some bread and milk as sustenance for the long journey, then rode alone to his destination.

He was a confident boy and had no trouble in negotiating with the buyer to get a good deal for the horse. And with his pockets lined with money he started the long walk home, spurred on by the pride he felt from his first horse sale.

That was the start of my father's horse dealing career, and from there he went on to get a real eye for a good horse, and even an eye for the not so good ones! One such horse was one he picked up from a local dealer; he got it cheap on account of the fact that the horse was lame, with four injured legs, so injured that the horse could not even stand. To anyone else that horse would have been a waste of money, a sure fire loss, but not to Daniel; he saw the potential in it. He took the horse home, and carefully tied its four legs up so that none of its legs were on the floor.

"We can get this better, Doll," he said to his wife as she looked on admiringly.

He tended to the horse's every need for a week, and in that time the horse's injuries began to heal.

Others would mock his efforts though, "What you doing now, Daniel?" they'd say, thinking the horse was good for nothing.

"You'll see," he'd reply, "Nothing has beat me yet!"

And he was right, after a while the horse started to drink and eat again, and through pure determination and a fascinating understanding of nature, Daniel nursed that horse back to a fine specimen of an animal. So fine in fact that he went on to sell it and got good money for it too.

My father loved horses and they loved him. I remember one time when my mother and father were pulled at Great Waltham with their horses; on the day before they were due to move away my father fed the horses and tied them to the wagon. Off to bed they went for the night, but in the morning one of the horses had gone. Dad looked up and down for his horse, but it was nowhere to be seen. Regretfully they still set off that morning as planned, travelling on without their lost horse. However, several months later whilst travelling back past Great Waltham where they had previously been stopping, my father drove past a children's park and noticed that there was a horse in there just like the one he had lost. As soon as he went over to it he recognised it as his own and jumped on its back and rode it back to where they were heading too; man and horse reunited once again.

My father had always had a way with animals; I remember him telling a story about an incident with a dog he once had. He'd been out and about in his horse and cart when his dog, a Lurcher, had caught a rabbit in one of the nearby fields. He was driving his cart down one of the lanes with his dog proudly carrying his prey in its mouth, when they were met by a policeman coming in the opposite direction.

"Pull over, boy," the policeman ordered.

Daniel did as he was told.

"Tell your dog to get that rabbit out of its mouth. I want it," the policeman said unashamedly.

Daniel had no fear of authority and he couldn't resist having a little game with the policeman.

"If you can get it, you can have it," he quipped.

The policeman was riled by his attitude but was up for the challenge and boldly walked over to the dog, bending over to pull at the rabbit in its jaws.

The dog just gripped tighter and growled at the policeman who was now looking rather red-faced.

Daniel smirked as the policeman yanked harder, and the dog responded with more menace, bearing as many of his sharp teeth as he could whilst still clutching hold of the rabbit.

"Stupid dog," the policeman muttered, embarrassed at his failed attempt to beat the animal. "Be on your way now, boy."

Daniel drove his horse and cart down the lane with the policeman following behind. It was a good five miles before the policeman turned off and when he did Daniel turned to his dog and softly and calmly said, "Drop the rabbit."

And it did.

I remember really laughing as my father retold that story, the glint in his eye still sparkling as he did.

It wasn't just animals that my father was at one with though. It was all of nature, he enjoyed being outside, especially if he was outside and making money at the same time. One of the other jobs he did quite a lot was laying turf; he made a reasonable living from it too, even laying the turf at Southend golf course, which had very strict standards. While he was there he didn't miss a trick and took it upon himself to dive into all of the pond areas to retrieve golf balls that had gone astray. (It was this diving into the depths of the murky ponds that caused him to have deafness in one ear.)

Over the years however the horse dealing became his life and he would travel miles if there was a good horse or a good deal at the end of his journey; he even rode bareback from Southend to Chelmsford for such a deal. The deals could and would happen anywhere and everywhere, with lots of traveller men choosing the pub as a good place to trade. One pub in particular was the Woodcutters in Southend; men would sit drinking into the evening as others brought horses into the pub, and paraded them around to seal a deal. It must have been a strange sight to behold but Daniel said that some of his best deals were carried out in that pub; perhaps the beer made people a little more willing to part with their money.

Daniel Buckley aged 18

As he grew from a boy to a man, my father developed his own sense of style too. He was a very old fashioned man with old fashioned values and tastes, and it was clear that he liked things just so. He always wore a trilby hat, cut just how he liked it, and dark brown corded trousers, no other colour or style would do. He would team them up with a long sleeve shirt, but if it had a collar or pockets on the front he would always cut them off before it went anywhere near his body. I'm not sure what it was he didn't like about them but he just didn't like them, and he'd always been that way. His feet would always be covered by dark brown lace up boots to go with his trousers. But interestingly he could never have shiny new boots; he didn't like new things, so he'd scrape new boots on the floor until they were sufficiently scuffed and tatty.

He had a determined attitude to wear what he wanted and to do what he wanted, and this was particularly evident when it came to him taking his driving test. They had had heavy rain that day and as a result the examiner refused to let him do his test because the roads were far too slippery. Daniel however couldn't see the problem; he scuffed his feet up and down the road a few times, before announcing, "I've driven horses in worse weather than this!" That was just how he was; straight talking and to the point. He had some interesting ways about him, but everyone knew where they stood with Daniel Buckley, and despite his ways, people couldn't help but like him. It was even said that if you couldn't get on with Daniel, you couldn't get on with anyone. And testament to that is the fact that he is still talked about and remembered fondly today and I will always be proud to call him my father.

Dolly

I was equally proud to be born to my mother, Dolly Buckley, who was also born and raised in Southend, Essex. She was one of ten children born to Rose and George Meecham. She had three sisters; Peggy, Betty and Joaney, and six brothers; Scuffy, Tottey, Billy, Jimmy, Michael and Wipett. As a young girl Dolly worked hard, starting out in a garden nursery, she also sold flowers and bagged moss and sold it to nurseries. She had a good business head on her shoulders and made money where she could.

Dolly and her family were not travellers though; they lived in a small house which was bursting at the seams with all twelve people battling for space. They had very little to do with travellers until one day when Dolly and her two sisters, Joaney and Betty, ventured into the woods near their family home. It was here that Daniel Buckley and other travellers were stopping in their wagons.

It was that evening that Dolly and Daniel first laid eyes on each other, and the spark of what would be a long and happy life together was ignited. It was in those woods that Joaney and Betty also met their future husbands, and their family became undeniably part of the traveller community.

Dolly and her friend Louie

It wasn't the perfect love story however, as the girls' mother, my grandmother, wasn't happy about them visiting the travellers.

"Don't you be going to those woods!" She'd say, "Don't get near those gypsies!"

But neither Dolly, Joaney nor Betty listened to her; they carried on visiting and carried on falling for their gypsy men. Dolly was strong willed and she didn't care that her mother didn't approve; she was in love and that was all that mattered.

When he was just twenty three years old Daniel arrived at Dolly's house one evening. She was merely nineteen, but he'd come to get her so that they could run away together.

Dolly's mother stood in the doorway pleading for her not to leave. Dolly wasn't a disobedient daughter but she was passionate, and she had always followed her heart. That night was no different; she packed up a few belongings and as she jumped up onto the horse and cart to leave, her mother's words ripped through that love filled heart;

"If you go, Dolly, you lay in your bed, there's no coming back here!"

Chapter 2

Determination

Despite her mother's warning Dolly and Daniel left there and then to start their lives together. The two young lovebirds didn't have much between them but with each other and a determination to make a success of their lives they travelled the roads in their wagon. Daniel dealt horses, sometimes leaving Dolly alone for two to three weeks at a time. It was a lonely time for her and she struggled to keep things ticking over while he was away, but when he returned with pockets full of cash and his arms open to embrace her, it all seemed worthwhile. Especially when his earnings meant she could splash out on some of her favourite foods like fish and chips or yum yum cakes, all washed down with a glass of Guinness to keep her iron levels up.

In 1940, the Second World War was really starting to take hold in England, with the dropping of bombs becoming normality. It was at this time that Daniel and Dolly were invited to move away to Wales, with a good friend Jim Lowe. It would have been safer for them, but Daniel refused, choosing instead to stand his ground within Essex. He was a determined man and he wasn't prepared to be uprooted because of the war.

(It wasn't until about nine years later that Jim and Daniel were reacquainted again. Daniel was stopping in Boreham at the time and the pair would meet up every Friday on market days. They would take the horse and carts to Victoria café in Chelmsford. Jim's son, Robbie Lowe, went on to marry Daniel's niece, Sheila, and to this day both families still see each other regularly.)

The war years made it tough for everyone back then, particularly when rationing hit, hitting some people very hard. But as a family we've always been quite resilient and found ways to make things work. I'll never forget a story my mum told me about one of the cunning ways she managed to get food for everyone. She went down to the local butchers in the village. There were lots of traveller women all waiting in a long queue hoping to get a morsel of meat for their families.

Dolly fetching water in Boreham

"Oh Dolly, you can't get any meat, we've been waiting in the queue for ages," one of them said, noticing my mother wasn't in the mood for queuing.

"Oh, I'll get some meat," she said confidently.

Dolly always had an idea or a trick up her sleeve, and that day was no different. She quickly adjusted her clothes and hair and made herself look a lot younger than her actual years, and she boldly walked past the queuing women and through the butcher's door.

"I've come to get my mummy's meat what she ordered," she said, in her most childlike voice.

The butcher looked at her and took pity on her, "Here you go, here's your meat," he said with a smile, handing over more than her fair share of rations.

Dolly walked out smiling much to the amazement of the other women still waiting patiently in line.

"I don't know how you done that, Dolly, but well done!" One of them said as Dolly walked by.

"I told you I would!" She grinned.

That's my mum all over.

Dolly and Mary as a baby

After a short time of married life, Dolly found she was expecting a baby and went on to have her first child, my eldest sister Lilly; she was a tiny baby when she was born and by all accounts my parents both doted on her. Dolly and Daniel were staying in Boreham near Chelmsford at the time, and the kind farmer were they were stopping used to allow Dolly to do her washing in one of the farm buildings, which was a Godsend! It gave her a break from struggling to do the washing outside over the fire. Daniel and Dolly led a simple life, with Dolly caring for their daughter and looking after their home, and Daniel going out on his bike collecting rabbit skins, fetching them home, and hanging them out to dry before taking them out to sell.

The couple were both very happy and they realised that raising a large family would bring them even more happiness and so they went on to have my three brothers and me, the youngest in the family. I've been told that when I was born there was an element of jealousy from Lilly as I'd ruined her reign as the only daughter, but she loved me all the same, and her and my three brothers were brought up to watch over me, as they still do today.

L-R: Daniel, Lilly, Johnny, Mark, Dolly and Richard

As young children Lilly and Mark went to Boreham School, although Mark didn't like school very much, so whilst Dad would drive Lilly there in the horse and cart, he and Mark would keep on driving and head over to Chelmsford market for the day... I think they both felt he would learn more from spending the day with Dad than he would in school.

As children we felt we had a blessed life, we had the countryside to roam in, we were surrounded by love, and our parents were teaching us lots of skills that would see us through life in the future.

Mary being held by cousin Billy

We did occasionally get up to mischief though, I recall one story of Lilly and my brothers helping themselves to a tin of treacle that they weren't supposed to touch. They were all tucking in when one of them noticed that Mum was coming back to the trailer. In the panic the tin of treacle was hidden... in Dad's bed, under the covers. His face was an absolute picture when he went to bed that night... but luckily he saw the funny side eventually!

My mum Dolly was a natural when it came to being a mother, and she was even a bit of an expert at delivering babies too. She brought so many babies into the world that it was hard to keep track of them all. Her midwife skills came in very handy, especially when my mother in law Aileen had her baby, Katie. She had her at home and if my mother hadn't been there to guide her through it then God only knows what would have happened. Aileen, like so many other women, will be eternally grateful for my mum's help in bringing their babies into the world.

Mum loved children in general, and it was whilst we were stopping in Kelvedon for a while that she befriended a young girl from the nearby children's home. The girl would stand at the railings chatting to us, and Mum, and the rest of us soon had a real soft spot for her. As our friendship with the girl grew, Mum and Dad decided they wanted to adopt her and bring her up as part of our loving family, rather than let her fester in that children's home. They put the wheels in motion and before long we were just weeks away from having a new sister in the family. Unfortunately, the fact that we were travellers stopped the process in its tracks. I'm not sure of the exact reason why but all I know is that right at the final stage of the adoption process we weren't deemed suitable to give this girl the loving family that she craved, and that we were willing to offer her. It was a sad day for all of us.

Dolly in her Austin A30 car

Mum had always wanted to help others, and one way she did that was through her gift of being able to tell fortunes. It was a skill that she used on many occasions, either reading tea leaves or using her crystal ball which she carried in a basket. I remember being about five years old when Mum took us down to The Angel pub in Kelvedon; we were too young to go in so we sat outside whilst Mum sat at one of the pub tables giving palm readings. Everyone appreciated Mum's talent for providing such accurate readings, and people were always coming to her for help and advice.

Daniel and Dolly Buckley were a phenomenal couple; talented, kind-hearted, hard-working and family orientated; and I and the generations that followed them have learned so much from the way they lived their lives. The one thing that stands out though is their determination... from Dolly's determination to get that piece of meat, or Daniel's determination to deal just one more horse, or their shared determination to raise a good, kind family. It was key to their happy life, and it's key to living life as a Romany gypsy.

Daniel, Lilly, Mark, Johnny, and Dolly holding Richard

Dolly at the Suffolk Show with a Stallion horse

Chapter 3

Life Lessons

As a family we are all hard workers; I was always helping out with jobs, as far back as I remember. In 1956 we spent some time staying on a farmer's land in Lindsell, Essex. The farmer was Mr Leader, a kind and generous man who went out of his way to help us. I remember quite clearly the excitement as he'd walk towards the wagon with his hands full of gifts; one day a brace of pheasants, the next a couple of rabbits. And in no time at all Mother would set to work adding ingredients to the large pot that was hanging sturdily over the fire, and she'd somehow convert his offerings into a hearty stew for all of us to enjoy. Mother was a great cook, and we'd all chip in to help her as and when we could. Mr Leader wasn't the only one who was generous to us; twice a week the local baker would call and give us a bag of mixed cakes. Although Mum would often ride her bike into the village when she needed to get some shopping, it wasn't always easy to do, especially with so many children to look after and so many other jobs to do; so we starting leaving a box out near the road for the baker, and he would leave a stash of tasty goodies in there for us. I loved the bakery box!

We rarely had treats which was why when the bakery box was full to the rim I was always so excited. We treasured these little moments and we treasured anything that was a little bit special. My sister, Lilly, had a very treasured possession, they were a pair of shiny red shoes. Mum had bought them for her as a gift, with strict instructions that they should only be worn on special occasions. However, one day, my cousin Sheila called round to see Lilly. Rather foolishly, Lilly made the decision to wear her special red shoes to play outside. She skipped and laughed as she ran across the field, playing merrily with Sheila, completely oblivious to the fact that her prize shoes were getting wet as she ran through the damp grass.

Noticing her error Lilly panicked, "Oh no! Look at my beautiful shoes… they're soaked!" she cried.

Sheila realised the trouble that Lilly would have been in if her mum had seen the state of the shoes, "Don't worry, I'll get these dry before your mum comes home," she said, reaching down to help Lilly out of her wet footwear.

Sheila had spotted the fire burning outside the trailer and that was when her brilliant plan had popped into her mind.

"Look," she said excitedly, "We'll just hang them over the fire; they'll soon dry off!"

Sheila and Lilly were both chuffed with their clever idea and were certain that Lilly would get away with it. That was, until the shoes slipped from their drying spot and fell into the orange flames below.

"No!" Lilly squealed, as Sheila used a stick to try and fish them out of the furnace.

"It's no good," Sheila said, admitting defeat, "It's too late; your shoes are ruined."

Lilly spent that evening nervously awaiting her mother's return. And as predicted, she was furious about the untimely demise of those beautiful red shoes.

"That's it girl," Mum said, "You won't be getting any more nice shoes like that if you can't look after them. You'll be wearing boots from now on!"

Lilly's sparkling red shoes were in stark contrast to the kind of attire I would wear. In my early years I was very much a tomboy. I didn't mind that I looked different to the other girls around me though. I was comfortable that way, and I had no desire to wear pretty dresses or bows in my hair. One of my friends did though; she was the epitome of what a little girl was supposed to look like. She had long straight hair, tied up with ribbons, and bows on her clothes, perfectly tied. For the most part, she and I got on well, despite our differences, but on one occasion our differences in opinion led to a rather heated argument; we tussled together and the bows in her hair came away in my clenched hand. It was against my normal reaction to things but I was so wound up that I couldn't control myself. I pushed her, straight into a muddy puddle. As the mud splashed onto her pretty dress the tears instantly fell onto her cheeks. As I watched her distraught little face sobbing I couldn't help but feel guilty but it was too late to apologise; the damage was done. The girl turned and ran back to her mother, clutching her bows and wailing as she ran.

I sheepishly made my way home to my mum and my brother, Richard. And as I knew would be the case, the little girl's mum, a woman named Holly, soon came over to speak to my mum.

"What has your little girl done to my daughter?" Holly asked, with rage in her eyes.

Cheekily, I replied, "I give her bow woo!"

Richard had always tormented me for not dressing like a pretty little girl, and in particular for not wearing bows, so it seemed appropriate that, that was my response.

I did apologise eventually though; once I'd swallowed my pride; and the two of us were soon playing happily together again.

Being the tomboy that I was I was always exploring the countryside. Whilst staying in Martin's Pit in Great Totham, we were fortunate to have a large duck pond just a few yards away from us. The ducks would wander around, minding their own business most of the time. As I meandered by them one morning I noticed that one of the ducks appeared to be in trouble. As I moved closer I realised that he'd swallowed a piece of string and was now choking on it.

I hated seeing animals in trouble and I ran as fast as I could to get my father.

"Dad, Dad, you need to come quick," I panted once I'd found him. "There's a duck in trouble, he's swallowed some string… he's choking!" I blurted out.

"Calm down love, I'll be right there."

Dad disappeared for a moment and returned yielding a needle and thread. We walked back to find the suffering duck and Dad very calmly knelt down, settled the duck and made a tiny incision in its neck. The cut was just big enough to allow him to pull the string free. And once he had, he used the needle and thread to stitch the duck's neck back together. Almost instantaneously the duck seemed back to its old self, and brought from the brink of death it merrily paddled off into the middle of the pond.

That was my first understanding of how fragile life was; that little duck was so close to taking his last breath.

From as far back as I can remember I'd always loved being around animals, and I particularly loved dogs, with one always by my side. Trixey was a small cocker spaniel who was white, black and brown in colour, and was a really faithful, family dog. But when I turned eight years old a new dog came into my life. My brother, Mark, had just finished working in the fields. He came up to the trailer with his overcoat wrapped tightly round his torso, and a smirk on his face that told me instantly he was up to something.

"I got you something, Babe," he said, looking pleased with himself. And before I had a chance to ask what, he opened his jacket and revealed a tiny ball of white fluff. From the fluff, two big eyes peered out at me and my heart skipped a beat. It was a mini poodle and I'd fallen in love with him right there and then. I named him Snowy and I took him everywhere with me. That was until the day I heard a big lorry pull up outside. I knew in my gut that something was wrong, and my instinct was correct. The lorry had hit poor Snowy, and my fluffy companion was dead. It took me a long time to get over the fact that he was gone and even though we got another dog, I still felt quite lost without him.

By the time I was nine I'd seen several animals facing death but on one terrifying day I saw a young traveller boy faced with his mortality. I and some of the other traveller children were playing outside whilst the adults sat around the fire chatting. Dad was there too, eating little sprat fish that had been fried in the pan… one of his favourite foods, along with spam and little winkle fish which he used a needle to help him get them out of the shell to eat.

All in all it was a day like any other; we were all having fun, enjoying the freedom of the countryside. The children ran, and we laughed, we chased each other and tormented each other, as kids did. A friend of ours, Pashey, had a little boy who was just five, he was running around with the rest of us, but he was also eating peanuts as he ran.

None of us realised the danger that he was in, until he stopped running and turned to face us. That was when we saw the look of terror in his eyes as he struggled to catch his breath. A peanut had become lodged in his throat, and as he clawed at his neck to try and find some air I could see the fear bubbling in his little face.

He ran to his mother who was still completely oblivious, talking around the fire. But one look told her exactly what had happened.

"He's choking!" I yelled. "Somebody help him!"

His mum instantly jumped to her feet and turned him over in an attempt to dislodge the stray peanut. It was no good, it was well and truly stuck.

"We need to get him to hospital!" his mother screeched, "Quickly!"

Everyone leaped into action, my dad jumping into the cab of his lorry and starting the engine and everyone else bundling themselves into the open back of the vehicle.

There were mumbles of concern as we all watched the poor little boy losing the battle against the peanut as we drove. His lips started to go blue, and then his whole body seemed to be tinged with a blue hue. It was extremely frightening, and none of us could say for sure that he'd pull through. We finally arrived at the front of the hospital and one of the men carried the boy into the front entrance, with the boy's mother crying by his side. The rest of us waited nervously for some news. It felt like an eternity before the mother's face appeared around the corner of the waiting room door, and even longer for her solemn face to break into a relieved smile. The hospital staff had saved him, the peanut had been freed, and no lasting damage had been done. In that moment life felt precious and I was even more grateful for my family and the love of our community.

Chapter 4

Work Hard, Play Hard

November of 1956 holds my first memory of Guy Fawkes night; I had no idea what to expect as we set out on the three mile walk to Lindsell village that night. Wrapped in as many layers as my mother could manage, I didn't feel the biting cold as it whipped through the air; my little face barely visible between the bottom of my hat and the spirals of my scarf. Before we even arrived in the village I could see the burning bonfire on the skyline. It was beautiful. I was used to fires, we lit one every night, but I'd never seen one on this scale. As we got closer I noticed the Guy balanced on top, the outline of his body slowly being taken over by the flames. It was amazing. We found a place serving hot soup and roasted chestnuts and the whole family tucked in to the warm delights before making our way back to our wagons.

But the 5th November was not just about Guy Fawkes night; it also signalled the start of the weather really turning. December was always the worst time for us. We still had to work in the fields, picking potatoes and pulling frost covered sugar beet. At times it was bitterly cold for those out there for hours at a time. I remember hearing others moaning that they couldn't hold the chopper to chop the sugar beet because their hands had gone numb from the cold that had hit their bones. We were always out working the land though, whatever the weather. The beat was often frozen to the ground making the job twice as hard as it should have been. But we did what we could to stay warm; my sister Lilly, my brothers Mark, John, and Richard, and my mum and dad all used to tie sacks around their waists for extra warmth and we wore socks on our hands to keep the biting cold from our fingertips.

Lilly pulling sugar beet

Thankfully, as I was only young I avoided the field work, but that didn't mean I sat at home idle. Instead I was given the responsibility of keeping the fire burning in a hedge nearby to where the rest were working. Quite a task for a five year old, but I rose to the challenge every day, knowing the importance of helping my family out, and providing somewhere for them to warm up when the temperature became too unbearable to work. My Father would come over and check I was alright every now and then, and he'd bring potatoes to put on the fire, so that everyone could eat that evening. I loved those potatoes, the smokiness of the flames still present as the butter melted over their fluffy insides. I'd have a sprinkle of salt on the top and it felt like heaven.

As we sat around eating our potatoes and drinking tea I could tell that everyone was tired and weary because they'd worked so hard. But even then they couldn't relax as once our mugs were empty we'd all have to gather our belongings and start our journey back home to our wagons, walking through wet ditches and navigating holes to get back to the trailer.

Being the little one it was tough for me to get over some of the ditches, but I managed. And when we finally arrived home everyone breathed a unanimous sigh of relief that another hard day was over.

My family also picked potatoes at a place called Hayley, near Bury St Edmunds. Once again I was too young to join in at the time, so I stayed at home and looked after two young babies who belonged to some other families staying with us; the parents were Nelson and Peggy, and Levi and Christine. I remember that we leant one of the families a small tent to sleep in, whilst the other set up home in the back of a lorry. I quite enjoyed looking after the babies, and I earned myself a bit of pocket money in the process. The rest of the family however worked long, hard days, picking potatoes from the black dirt and placing them into their baskets. The tractor, with its trailer being pulled behind, would follow their route, driving up and down the field, stopping by each of them so that they could pass their baskets up to the man in the trailer. He would empty out the produce and pass the basket back for them to start all over again. Sometimes the potato picking process involved clamping the potatoes. This meant they were picked, covered with straw and then buried under soil in order to keep them fresh for the winter. It was an arduous process but we never complained; hard working is all we know.

At the end of a long day picking potatoes everyone was guaranteed to be exhausted but the farmer would still expect them to do more. Their final job would be picking arrows (the name for the potatoes that had been left in the ground). The farmer would give the arrows to his animals or sometimes to us, if he was feeling generous.

It would be getting dark by the time everyone made their way back home from the fields, and once there they would wash off the dirt from the day and get to bed as soon as they could, to rest, ready to do it all again the next day.

Winter felt like an eternity for me when I was younger as everyone else was always out working and I had to spend a lot of time on my own. Thankfully I had a loyal companion to help me wile away my days and keep me company. I had Sandy, a beautiful Labrador dog who was never far from my side. Sandy and I used to take ourselves off across the fields and walk for miles. It's a shame that kids can't have that kind of freedom nowadays, and that's one thing I'll always be appreciative of, the fact that I could just go off and explore, and feel safe doing it.

On one occasion I went exploring with my brother Richard and one of my cousins. We would often go out together looking for treasure. If we found old coins we'd take them home and clean them up with brown sauce, before stashing them away to spend on a special treat once we'd saved up enough money. On this particular occasion however, we walked for a few miles and hadn't found much before we came across a house that we'd never noticed before. We were all pretty tired and thirsty, so we knocked on the front door and waited. After a short while a lady answered our knock; she had a kind face and seemed glad that she'd got some visitors. She invited us in and we sat down at her kitchen table whilst she made us all a drink.

"Would you like to see my cellar?" she asked after we'd finished with all our introductions.

"Yeah," Richard said excitedly. He jumped up from his chair, and we followed his lead.

As we stepped down into the cellar we could see why the lady was so proud of it. It was stocked from floor to ceiling with bottles and barrels full of homemade wines and brews. She could have opened up a shop she had so many.

After a while we realised we needed to be heading home if we were going to make it back before dark, especially as the nights were really drawing in.

"Wait!" the woman said as I stepped outside the front door. "One moment; I've got a gift for you." And with that she turned and rushed back into her lounge.

I could tell she'd taken a shine to me from the moment she answered the door, but I hadn't expected that she'd give me a gift.

"I wonder what it is," I whispered to the boys.

"Probably a doll or something rubbish," my brother replied.

When she returned she was holding a small box. It was dark on the outside and rather uninviting, but when she opened up the lid, inside stood a beautiful fairy, that moved elegantly in circles, in time with the delicate jingling music that the box played. It was beautiful, and once the fairy had completed her dance I couldn't wait to wind up the key and watch her perform all over again. I was mesmerised and overwhelmed that she'd given me such a beautiful gift.

I kept that music box for years, a reminder of my carefree childhood and the kindness of strangers.

Chapter 5

Life in Stebbing

We'd survived another bleak winter and as spring of 1958 started to roll in, my sister, Lilly, started to get a bit of a spring in her step too… she started courting.

He was a young boy named Moe. He lived in Ipswich but that didn't deter him travelling the forty-mile bus journey from his home to Stebbing, where we were at the time. Stebbing was a lovely little village, it was my birthplace and where I'd spent most of my young life so far. My brothers were all Essex-born too but they were born near Rodings, about ten miles South of Stebbing.

I remember Lilly getting so excited when she knew Moe was coming to visit. He would normally come on a Saturday morning and she would run down the road to meet him from the bus. It was a relationship that naturally blossomed and everyone could see that they were meant to be together. After two years, in 1960, they made it official, with a beautiful wedding at a registry office in Great Dunmow. I can remember my sister beaming as she fulfilled her role as the blushing bride perfectly. She wore a smart red suit with a crisp white blouse; she looked lovely. It was actually a double wedding, as Moe's sister, Buncy married a young man named Tommy on the same day, and all of our families and friends helped them celebrate with a traditional reception at the White Hart pub. I remember we all walked to the pub from the registry office, and I walked with my friends Celia and Lizzy, even the bride and groom were on foot… there were no flash wedding cars back then! Today a posh car or a horse and carriage are considered the minimum requirement for a respectable wedding. But nothing about the weddings of today really reflects the way we used to celebrate a couple getting wed; things were a lot simpler back then. When a couple got married they would go to their local registry office and then back to the pub for a drink up and food. Today, no wedding is complete without a guest list of two to three hundred people, decorated tables and chairs, table centrepieces; I've even seen light up dance floors! It's a world away from Lilly and Moe's wedding.

Once she was married, Lilly left our trailer and her and Moe got a little trailer and a dormavell van of their own. We'd only upgraded from a wagon to a trailer the year before and it felt like real luxury to me. But Lilly was keen to move out and seemed very happy when they moved into a field amongst other travellers in High Easter, not far from Chelmsford. I missed her once she'd gone though; she was like a second mum to me, so I was pleased whenever she suggested I went to stay with them for a day or two.

I got on really well with Moe's family, his mother, Nelly and his father, Sonny were so welcoming to all of us, and I called them Granny and Grandfather because that's how they felt to me; plus all of my real grandparents apart from Granny Rose, my mum's mother, had sadly all passed away by this time.

With Lilly gone, a lot of her roles fell to me. One of the jobs which I loved doing was getting the food shopping. I'd never been to school so I couldn't read or write, but I found my own way to remember the things my mother asked me to get. Whenever she'd recite a shopping list to me I'd simply draw the items on a bit of paper so that I could look at the pictures once I got to the shop and recall every single item correctly. It worked every time.

As time went on Lilly and Moe had a son, Sonny, and I spent more and more time at theirs, helping to look after him, especially when Lilly and Moe were out working in the fields. I was only about eleven at this stage but I loved playing mother, it gave me a purpose, and I enjoyed preparing dinner for when the workers got home... I could make a beautiful pheasant stew which always went down a treat.

Sonny was the apple of all our eyes, he was a very good looking little boy and one day whilst Lilly was out working my mother decided that she would attempt to cut his hair. It was a decision she probably went on to regret. Sonny refused to sit still, and as Mother attempted to carry out a perfect basin cut, his constant wriggling meant it was never going to turn out well.

We all stood in silence, with our mouths open wide as we inspected his new style. It was completely lopsided, with chunks missing from one side and long strands hanging down on the other.

"Oh, it'll grow again," Dolly said with a smile.

Lilly wasn't best pleased with the cut, but she knew her boy's beautiful locks would soon grow back; and thankfully they did.

I loved spending time with my family, and September in particular was always a special time for me. As a family we'd travel to Kent and go hop picking with other travellers. As we worked during the day, the smell of the hops were beautiful, and at night we would settle down round the fire and laugh, joke and tell stories; the men having a good drink and a smoke, late into the night.

The family hop picking

There were some little chalets near to where we were staying, with non-travellers in. My mother and father told us to stay away from them and not torment the people staying there, but they actually came to enjoy us being there and they eventually joined in with us round the fire one evening.

One day I walked past their doorstep and I took a bottle of milk. I brought it home and my mother went crazy at me… she knew how to tell me off good and proper!

My mum could be stern like that but she also had a great sense of humour and every April fool's day she would give my dad a cup of hot water instead of a cup of tea, and she fooled him every single time!

Romany Glossary

English	Romany
Pound	Bar
Man	Chavy
Woman	Mort
Dog	Duke
Horse	Grie
Farmer	Roy
Gun	Yog
Wood	Cosh
Food	Scran
Eyes	Yoks
Hands	Morelos
Hair	Bore
Clothes	Togs
Good	Cushty
Stopping place	Hatching tan
Shoes	Chokkas
Me	Mandi
Wagon	Vardo

Chapter 6

Settling Down

One of the things that really stuck in my mind from my childhood was going to visit my Uncle Billy's wife, Phoebe, after she'd had her babies. I'd seen babies before but these were special, they were quads, something that was very rare to see. They had two boys and two girls and they were perfect bundles of innocence. Their arrival was such a rarity that it even made the local news as broadcasters were as keen as I was to tell people about the four little miracles.

But in amongst the excitement of marriages and births, day to day life continued with the monotony of field work. All of us working hard, and my mother seemingly working harder than any other traveller woman I'd ever come across. It was the way she was though; she wanted to provide for her family and make sure everything was just right.

Not every day went to plan though; I remember that one morning my sister Lilly was getting ready to go to work. She stood and boiled some hot water so that she had some to put in her flask to keep her warm during the long cold day ahead, but as she poured the water into the flask she had a momentary loss of concentration and she missed the flask and poured it straight into her welly boot; unfortunately she was wearing it at the time! We rushed her to hospital and they managed to get her boot off but it left poor Lilly with scarring on her foot. She was soon back out to work though; we could never stay idle for long.

After a while we started travelling with another family from Kent; Levi and Louie, we all got on well and we travelled together for some time before we finally stopped in High Easter, on a corner known as 'starved man's corner', so named because it was believed it was practically impossible to earn a living around there. But not so for my father; he could always make a living.

Southend Hospital Welcome Four Celebs - The Meecham quads were born in Southend Hospital's maternity department on 3rd January 1962 and were hardly out of the national media. They made headlines around the country when they were born.

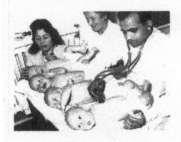

Edward, Christopher, Lucy and Yana – who were conceived naturally - made an instant family for Phoebe Meecham, who already had eight-year old Ronnie.

The four became overnight celebrities – they were asked to open Colchester Zoo, modelled to advertise Cow and Gate baby products and were besieged by press photographers at every birthday.

Newspaper coverage of the quadruplets' birth

While my father went out dealing with horses, my mother would be left with the trailer and sometimes the police would come and move them along. But with Dad being away my mother had no way of telling him where they were going. To combat this problem, between them they invented a plan that If they did get moved she would leave a lump of turf to indicate which way she had gone at each road junction. It was ingenious and their system didn't fail them once

We stayed in High Easter over Christmas; our Christmas celebrations were nowhere near as extravagant as they are today, and we never had that much in terms of presents or food, but we made the most of what we did have. And unlike today, we didn't have long extended Christmas breaks either. Boxing day morning would see everybody getting up and getting straight back into their normal work routine. This particular year, on Boxing Day morning we were on the move again; this time to Little Totham, twenty miles away. My father had bought a piece of land there from a man named Billy Twin. He paid £72 for one third of an acre. The land itself was very run down and overgrown; to one side of the land there was an old carriage, which Billy Twin used to live in but other than that there wasn't much else. There was no running water and no electricity, but as always, we made do with a gas bottle in the trailer and a good old fire outside.

From the moment we arrived we knew this was going to be our stopping place, a permanent home; but neither me, nor the other children in the family were happy about it. We didn't want to settle down, and especially not there. But despite our reluctance we all had to chip in to try and make this piece of derelict land home, particularly as Dad had reached an age where he couldn't keep up with all the travelling. He was ready to settle down.

We cut trees down to make a base for the trailer to sit within. Being winter, we hadn't made it easy for ourselves as there was ice and snow on the ground making it hard to clear a space, but through pure determination and hard work, we managed.

Eventually we started to settle, and we got a water connection going and electricity too, it took a while but we got there in the end. But even when we'd got an electricity supply there were some things that were still best done the old fashioned way; one of those being Mother's cooking. Her meat puddings and stews were just delicious, especially cooked over the fire in a pot, hanging from a hook. There was no doubt in my mind that food just tasted better cooked that way. I loved my mother's cooking but one of my favourite dishes was her pancakes, which used her very own cooking method. She'd whip together some flour, raisins and milk to make the batter, then she fried them in lard; once they were cooked she tossed them onto a plate and sprinkled lashings of sugar on top. They were so lovely, they make my mouth water just thinking about them now!

In the early days in Totham the family made a living any way they could. One such way was by picking peas for the farmer. We spent many long days picking, sorting and bagging peas, and our bodies would physically ache at the end of the day. But it was all worth it once the farmer heaved the bags, bulging with peas, onto the scales. All eyes would be on him, watching to see just how much each bag weighed, which of course, in turn meant just how much us hard workers would be paid. Payment wasn't always in cold hard cash though… frequently we would be rewarded with a live chicken! It would always kick up a bit of a fuss when it was handed over though, as if it knew its destiny. We would tie a piece of string around its neck, like a lead, and then the animal would be walked back home, where mother would prepare it ready to provide a hearty dinner.

Daniel and Dolly cleaning scrap metal

Another way my family made a living was by logging, and collecting rags and iron scrap, but eventually, by the summer months my father had started a landscape gardening business and he was earning a steady income. I helped him whenever I could, although it was hard work; one particular job which I struggled with was laying turf. My brother Johnny helped with this job too, cutting the turf, rolling it out, and rushing back and forth delivering it to all our customers. I'd have to pull a very big roller, at least three foot high, in order to roll the turf to make a lawn. I know my father appreciated my efforts though and I felt proud when I saw the finished garden looking immaculate thanks to our hard work.

Daniel and his water cowells

As well as his business, my father had a passion for old ringers and ploughs; he spent much of his free time painting them different colours and making them good. He'd even put signs on them with sayings like 'hard times' or 'old fussy'. They drew quite a bit of attention, and people would stop and look at them in amazement if they happened to be driving by. People were so interested in fact, that a reporter from the local press even came by to do an interview with him, to find out more about his restored treasures.

My father was always tinkering with something, and he had lots of tools in order to get the job done properly. However, he didn't trust us to look after his tools or to put them back if we borrowed them, so much so that eventually he started hiding his tools from us!

Daniel with the local newspaper reporter

As well as machinery, my dad also looked after horses, even finding time to help my brother Mark with his horses which he kept on the common land next to our land. My mother was a lover of horses too. Her prized horse was named Marney; she was a beautiful brown mare, and when Mum sat on her back it was as if they were thinking and moving as one. She loved that horse and that love shone through in the way she rode her, and the way Marney responded to her directions. Mother could do absolutely anything she wanted when sat astride Marney, from tricks to riding bare back; nothing was beyond the pair of them.

We were all starting to get used to life in Little Totham, but after a couple of years there it was time for another family member to leave the nest. My brother, Mark, had met a traveller girl called Una. As quickly as Lilly's relationship had flourished so did theirs and they soon married and moved away before starting their own family. That just left me and my two brothers at home to help our parents. My brother Richard then went on to meet his wife, Lena, and they too married, moved away and had children. I was jealous of Lena for a while, she was only a few years older than me and she'd taken my brother away and started a life for herself, while I was stuck at home, working hard, and feeling more and more abandoned as more and more children flew the nest.

Obituaries

Dannie collected antiques from the scrapyard

DANNIE BUCKLEY, whose collection of old farm implements, antique mangles and other relics have intrigued passers-by at Office Lane, Little Totham, for years, has died aged 71.

At his funeral at St Mary's, Kelvedon, yesterday (Wednesday), seven limousines took members of his extensive family to the church.

For years Dannie and his wife Doris were travellers, moving around the countryside with a horse and wagon, working on farms and known for their skill in breaking in horses, and caring for sick ponies.

They settled in Little Totham 20 years ago, where they began to exhibit Dannie's collection of antiques outside his caravan home.

Dannie greatly prized his collection, which he had gathered together throughout his life, saving many intriguing antiques from the scrapyard. The collection included old mangles, which would make washday a nightmare for any modern housewife, ancient ploughs, water-carriers, bird scarers, and carts. All were lovingly cared for and kept in order by Dannie.

He met his wife Doris when she was 19, and he came to her door selling mats. She too is well known for her skill with sick animals, and especially for her herbal cures.

The couple had three sons, and two daughters and there are seventeen grandchildren.

Dannie Buckley with his old ploughs and mangles.

Woodyard worker for

His work remembered in an Obituary in the local paper

Thankfully for me though, my brother John didn't marry until quite a bit later, in the 1970s, so I didn't feel totally deserted growing up. John and his wife Silvey also went on to have their own children, so I ended up with a lot of nieces and nephews.

Little Totham definitely had its perks though, one of them being Eddie King. He lived just down the lane with his mother, brothers and sisters in a derelict cottage.

I didn't know it then but Eddie was the man I was going to marry.

I didn't know it because at that time I had absolutely no interest in boys, in fact, I hated them. And I particularly hated Eddie. When I was about twelve, I even ran him over on my bike, and when we were forced to sit next to each other in the cab of my dad's lorry I would always turn my back on him, just in case he attempted to make conversation with me.

However, as time went on boys suddenly became more appealing and my sisters helped me with my clothes and make-up so that I could finally ditch the tomboy look. My new look certainly caught the attention of Eddie. At first I played it cool, he would drive into the yard, and make a beeline for me.

"You gonna make a cuppa for me?" he'd yell from his cab.

"Nope, no time," I'd reply coyly.

But he could tell I was just playing with him, and after a while he plucked up the courage to approach my dad and asked him if he could take me out. My dad's response? "Her brothers won't be happy! If you can get through them you can take her out!"

He was right, my brothers weren't too happy. They were very protective of me and they were all against us starting a relationship. It was only Mum, Dad and Lilly that were happy for us in the early stages so we kept our meetings pretty secret in the beginning.

As our relationship flourished I realised that I needed a bit more independence, and I knew that one way I could achieve that was by learning to drive. I was seventeen when Eddie gave me my first lesson; I couldn't afford to pay for professional lessons so Eddie took me to the aerodrome and very patiently taught me everything I needed to know. It was a struggle for me at times, but I was determined, and when I put my mind to something that's all it takes to achieve it. After a lot of hard work I passed my test first time, in a mini truck. I was so proud of myself and excited about what it meant to hold a driving licence. I could come and go as I pleased; I had the independence that I'd craved. Although it wasn't all plain sailing as I didn't actually have a car of my own, but if I needed to go somewhere it was always easy enough to 'borrow' Dad's truck.

If it hadn't been for Eddie I don't think I would have had the courage to take that driving test, he was a great help to me and over time we became very close. He was a great help to my family too, even helping my father out with his work when he needed a hand.

Dad didn't seem to stop working, on a Saturday he would go out on his rounds taking logs to sell door to door. He had regulars that he would visit in the local villages and the pensioners that he served relied on him, especially in the winter. He would normally deliver five bags of logs to each customer at a time; he used old fertilizer bags collected from the local farmers to pack the logs into. He was always generous with his logs too and his loyal customers really appreciated his generosity. So much so that when another family started trying to sell logs, Dad's customers refused to buy from them.

Dad's round didn't always go smoothly though, one Saturday afternoon he'd taken my sister Lilly out with him, and as they walked up to a house with their bags of logs, a large Alsatian dog leapt from the house and jumped up onto Lilly's back. Lilly screamed, Dad shouted and the dog snarled as everyone fought to get the dog off her. When he finally retreated it was clear that Lilly had been hurt, and on closer inspection Dad saw that the dog had taken a chunk out of her back. As soon as Dad saw the dog had drawn blood, he saw red. The rage bubbled inside him and he let it out in a fierce rant at the dog's owner, a small woman, now stood defiantly at her front door with the dog by her side.

"We could have you us people!" Dad shouted as he backed away down the path before his rage got away with him.

Back at home, our mother, Dolly, cleaned Lilly's wound with salt water and dressed it with Dettol cream. She was all for going to get this woman but Dad and Lilly convinced her to let it lie.

That wasn't the first time that a dog had caused mayhem on the log round. One particular Saturday a dog ran out in front of Dad's truck and swerving to avoid it he and his truck finished up in a ditch. A few weeks later he and Eddie were once again out on the very same log round, driving exactly the same route. This time Dad was driving a bit too fast and taking a corner with a bit more gas than he should have done and he struggled to keep control once more, "I nearly done it again," he said. Thankfully he eased off the accelerator for the rest of the journey and they both made it home in one piece.

Eddie helped Dad as much as he could and our relationship grew stronger and stronger. As our love grew, even my brothers could see what a good man he was, and after five years of courting, he proposed to me.

Chapter 7

A New Life

It was 1971 when Eddie and I got married at the local registry office. I was just twenty and after the wedding we moved straight into a trailer of our own. I felt uneasy about married life to start with, I missed my Mum, and after just one week I went back to see her for the day. She could tell instantly that I was homesick, and not particularly enjoying the role of wife; but she was firm with me, and told me in no uncertain terms that I had to go home to my husband and get on with married life.

And that's exactly what I did. After a couple of years I discovered I was expecting a baby and I was really excited about becoming a mum. I worked for the full nine months, right up to the very last moment. It was April and as I stood there, in the middle of the field, I felt a pain. It was a pain like nothing I'd ever felt before. My mother was stood nearby and she saw the look on my face as the pain gripped me.

"I think you better get to hospital now Mary, that's where you need to be."

She was right of course; I was ready to have my baby. Eddie, who was also at work at the time, dropped everything to drive me to hospital in Maldon, Essex. And later, in the early hours of the morning, our first daughter, Josephine, arrived.

The labour and being a mother was all very new to me, as was being in hospital. I'd never been to hospital before, not even when I was born as I was born in a wagon, as we all were back in that time.

I didn't like being in hospital; I felt claustrophobic being trapped within those four clinical walls. I was used to being outside and working in the fields; I liked my freedom, and really wasn't used to being inside any building for a length of time and especially not a hospital.

In those days women were expected to stay in hospital for ten days after they had their baby. All of the other new mums spent their days nursing their babies and reading magazines. But I couldn't join in with their routine because I was illiterate. I couldn't read or write; I'd never learnt how and up to that point I had always got by without it. Sitting in my hospital bed I flicked the pages of the magazines that were piled on my bedside table. But I was only looking at the pictures; the words meant nothing to me. It was during those ten long days that I realised that I no longer wanted to just get by; I wanted to learn to read and write.

But first I had to get back to my normal life. Those ten days were awful for me and you can imagine how frustrated I was at the end of that time. I was desperate to get back to my way of life, and to the comforts of my trailer. Eddie had prepared everything for Josephine and I including transforming one of the cupboards from the trailer into a cot for the baby. Once I was home I had lots of people supporting me; I had the help of my mum, sister and sister in-laws, but I was keen to get back to the life I was used to, and so within a week of being home I was out working in the field once again, with Josephine in the pram by my side.

It was a scorching hot, sunny, May and we were out in the fields chopping sugar beet. Little Josie had the protection of an umbrella over her pram but I and the rest of the family were at the mercy of the blazing sunshine all day as we walked up and down the rows of beet.

I would see to Josie when she needed me, either changing nappies, which in those days were cloth or a piece of towel cut down to size and secured with a safety pin. (Disposable nappies weren't even an option back then, so each cloth nappy would be washed by hand and used again.) And once she was clean I'd settle her in her pram and get back to work. I didn't even stop to feed her myself I simply propped her bottle up and she sucked away until she'd had her fill. There was no time to sit down and savour the moment or even to take a minute's rest; we all had to work hard to earn money and that was just how it was.

Things have changed a lot since those days though; people have more time to sit and play with their babies, they can take time to take them out for leisurely walks and meet other babies and other new mums. But back then there was no time for any of that; even though we loved the children very much, we knew that working and earning money had to be our priority. However, we did our best to make use of what little time we did have with them at night, playing with the children and taking time to nurture them before bedtime.

Things were very different to the way they are now. For example, if you look at the babies of today their clothes, toys and accessories are all so much nicer than anything we could have given our children. Today's traveller babies are dressed in the finest clothes, with beautiful frills and bows for the girls, and smart outfits for the boys. And it's not just the clothes that are superior; the prams, bottles, cots and other items are so much more luxurious than anything we used to have. There is one pram in particular, a beautiful Silver Cross pram, which is highly desired amongst new traveller mums, and something that I could have only dreamt of for my children. We simply couldn't afford any of those things back then, we worked hard and earned a living, but it was spent wisely on essentials; the trailer which Eddie and I lived in back then was one that he'd bought for fifty pounds! If only things were that cheap nowadays!

We worked all year round so that we could continue putting food on the table, but as the cold weather set in it made working conditions hard again, but we never let it beat us. One November a farmer from Hatfield Peverel asked me, my sister-in-law Lena, and my mother, to pick up the potatoes that were left over from October, because of the wet weather. It was a bitter November, with frost on the ground and snowflakes turning the air a misty white.

We worked as we always did though, not letting the freezing temperature get the better of us. At dinner time we all helped to build a small fire in a little spinney, which allowed us the luxury of some heat for a few minutes at least. We sat soaking up the warmth only for us to realise that the extreme temperatures had caused Mum's wellies to start to fall apart!

But even Mum's failing footwear didn't stop us working and we carried on until we'd picked every last potato from the cold ground. It was a hard day's graft and we were glad when it was over, but it was worth every second, especially as we got paid extra at the end of the day.

We worked hard and I was taking care of my little family, and life was good. But as time went on I remembered the promise I'd made to myself whilst in hospital with Josephine; I needed to learn to read. It wasn't an easy battle by any means, but through hard work and evening classes, I went on to realise that ambition. I studied at Thurstable School in Tiptree; it was a big step to bring myself to walk into that classroom on my first day in September. It was a big school and I felt totally out of my depth. The anxiety surged through my body as I anticipated who my classmates would be and what my teacher would make of me. I wondered whether he'd ever taught anyone with so little reading skills as me. I needn't have worried though; my teacher was a lovely man called John Ashley and he inspired me to succeed. Of course, the fact that my sister and the rest of my family were all so supportive helped my cause. My sister-in-law, Lena, even felt inspired by me and she joined the class too, working alongside me to conquer our fears and finally learn to read and write. Sadly, John died of a sudden heart attack and it left me wondering whether I'd be able to do quite so well under the instruction of a new teacher. The new teacher came in the form of a woman called Pauline. She had a very different style to John and it took me a few weeks to get used to her approach. But eventually we learned to understand each other and she continued to help me in my quest for literacy. She was a great motivator for me, even putting me forward to undertake a first aid course. It was a massive challenge, and with much regret I missed the last two weeks of the course, meaning I didn't officially complete it. That's one of my only regrets; I wish I'd had the tenacity to finish it.

My sister in-law Lena and I spent quite a lot of time together; one crisp morning as the sun was only just starting to show its face, we headed out together to pick beans. It was five a.m. and we knew that Mr Godwin, the farmer, would be waiting for us at his farm in Little Totham. He was a nice man, always friendly, and always praising us for the hard work we did.

When we arrived we walked straight over to the tractor, as we always did, in order to get some empty boxes to store the day's pickings. As we approached the tractor we noticed something on the driver's seat. It was a large bag and as we got nearer our instincts told us that it wasn't just any old bag.

"Take a look then," Lena urged me.

I didn't need telling twice. I climbed up to the seat and opened the top of the bag to peer inside. I gasped as I realised what we'd stumbled across... a bag full of money!

"It's stashed full," I called down to Lena, "Notes, coins... it must be all of yesterday's takings!"

For a split second Lena and I hesitated about what we should do with our find, but a moment later, looking straight at each other I could see that we had both come to the same decision. We had to hand the money back to Mr Godwin.

We were honest people, and he was a good man so there was no way we could consider doing anything but the right thing. I scooped up the bag and carefully climbed down from the tractor. Together we marched the bag to the farmer's house, like two security guards with the crown jewels.

As we reached the front door we were met by one of the farmer's sons. We didn't know his name but I'd seen him many times.

"Err, is your dad there?" I asked, "We have something that belongs to him," I stated, feeling a sense of pride at our good deed.

"I'll get him," he said, running back into the house.

It seemed like a long wait before Mr Godwin appeared.

"Hello there," he said, looking puzzled as to why we weren't already hard at work.

"We have something here we think you should have," Lena chipped in quickly.

I passed him the bag full of money, beaming as I did so.

"Oh yeah, thanks for that," he said, before turning to walk back into his house. He didn't even open the bag to check it was all there! I guess he trusted us; and rightly so.

We turned away and walked to the field to start our day's work.

"Do you think he was pleased we'd brought it back to him," I asked Lena as we filled our first box of beans.

"I think so," she said thoughtfully.

"Maybe we'll get a reward," I said excitedly.

"You never know," Lena grinned back, "We'll just have to wait and see, I guess."

We waited… all day, but the reward never came.

The lack of reward didn't stop me doing what was right when a similar situation occurred again though. I was driving along with my mum and my oldest daughter in the back seat, when I spotted something on the side of the road. I slowed down to get a closer look. It was a briefcase. I stopped the car, got out, walked over to the abandoned briefcase and picked it up. There wasn't a lock on it so I opened it up and looked inside.

Daniel playing with his grandchildren

"I can't see a name or anything," I said to my mum.

"Let's just take it home and sort it out there," she replied.

When we got home I had another look through all the paperwork inside. There were letters, cheque books, credit cards and all sorts of documents, but I still couldn't find any contact details for the owner. After a day I had one last look and found a phone number. The man on the other end was so grateful that we'd picked it up, that when he came to collect it from our home, this time we did get a small reward.

We experienced a few interesting events whilst out driving, one which amused us all occurred one foggy night in 1964, my father and his friend and neighbour, Morris, were driving back from the pub. The fog was so thick that Dad couldn't see which direction he should be driving in to get home. He drove round and round the common, trying to get his bearings, and he'd probably have been doing that until morning if my brother hadn't spotted him and pointed him in the right direction. It gave us all a good laugh though!

Daniel playing golf in the yard

Life in Little Totham was pretty perfect for all of us now, I had my own little family and my parents were enjoying seeing their family grow. My father loved children and he was in his element when he was surrounded by his grandchildren.

But whilst he loved playing with his grandchildren, Daniel was even more delighted when he was surrounded by both grandchildren *and* horses… his two great passions. He'd broken in many horses over the years, taming them and training them to be the obedient, calm natured animals that were part of the family.

When Josie, my eldest daughter was playing outside one day, Dad called over to her.

"Come over 'ere, Josie!"

Josie came running, excited to see what her grandfather had to say.

"I need you to do me a favour. Bend down for me so this horse can jump over your back."

Josie turned up her nose. She didn't want to do it; the thought of what could happen if the horse didn't make the jump, really frightened her.

Her grandfather noticed the fear in her eyes. "Don't be silly, get here now and do it!" He said firmly.

Josie did as she was told and nervously bent over. She closed her eyes tight as my dad pulled the horse's lead and led it clean over Josie's back. Josie was relieved to say the least, and Dad was happy that yet another horse was coming along nicely.

Chapter 8

New Ventures

In July 1976 I was pleased to be expecting my second child. It was a very hot summer that year and I was somehow still working out in the fields picking peas. I persevered with my work, putting in full days then driving myself back to the trailer, the heat of the day along with the increasing discomfort I was feeling, really starting to take its toll. Back at the trailer all I could think was that I needed to cool down my hot, swollen feet. So I took a bowl of cold water and breathed a sigh of relief as I relaxed my feet into it.

When I finally went into labour I drove myself to the hospital in Maldon, Essex, and met Eddie there; later that afternoon my son Karl arrived. As with Josephine I had to stay in hospital for ten long days. Eddie visited me in the evenings but during the days he would be out at work, earning the money needed to support our little family. Thankfully my sister Lilly minded Josephine for me until I was allowed back home.

Karl and I were home just a week before it was time for me to get back to work again. It was the same routine as when I had Josephine; Karl would be in his pram while I worked, and this time Josephine would merrily play with a bag of toys that she had, keeping herself amused until the day's grafting was up.

I carried on working in the fields for another ten years after this, but then one day the farmer told us that it would be the last year, as machines were to be taking over our roles; labour was no longer required as the machinery could do our jobs a lot quicker and cheaper than we could.

It was a shock for all of us but we didn't let it deter us; we could always find a way to make money. I went on to pick crab apples off the trees instead and elderflowers too during the summer months. Once we picked them we would then bag them up and drive to Tiptree, Essex, to the world renowned jam factory, they would then weigh the fruit and pay us accordingly. It kept us going for a good while.

During the winter months I needed another source of income and that was when I discovered my talent for making holly wreaths. It was a great job for me, especially as I could get on with it whilst Karl and Josie were at school.

I've never shared my secret to making them until now…

Mary's Holly Wreaths

1. The process starts in January/February; this is when you need to collect hazel sticks, just before they start budding.
2. Once you've found your sticks you need to cut them off so that they're approximately four foot long.
3. Take the sticks back home and bend them to make a circle shape and then leave them hung up until the autumn.

Creating the circle of hazel sticks

4. The next step is to collect grass or straw to twine around the hoop. You can then hang up the wreaths in bunches of twenty-five until December.

Adding twine to the hoop

5. The crowning glory on any wreath is of course the holly. Pick the holly and berries in bundles and then tie the holly onto the wreaths with some garden string to create a beautiful, traditional holly wreath.

Adding berried holly to the wreaths

6. Once my wreaths were assembled I would drive to the shops and market to sell them. I was confident that they would all be bought, especially as the shops would always put their orders in well in advance.

Earning money and working hard was in our blood. The work never stopped for any of us, even for dear old Mum who, by the 70s was really not a well woman. But that didn't stop her, she'd still march out to the strawberry fields, sometimes as early as five 'o'clock in the morning. She was cunning like that; going out that early meant she would be able to get to the best row of strawberries before anybody else. By the end of the day she would have boxes full of them, ripe and juicy. The farmer appreciated her hard work and he trusted her to write down exactly how many boxes she'd filled each day. But as I said, Mum was cunning to the last, and she would always sneak one or two extra digits onto her totals. With figures like that in the book, the other strawberry pickers couldn't help but admire Mrs Buckley for her record breaking day's work.

Chapter 9

Gypsy Traditions

As a community, gypsy travellers have a lot of respect for the traditions that their ancestors established. These traditions largely dictate the way in which travellers live *and* die. Although, not all of the traditions have stood the test of time; but a lot do still stand, some of these relate to what happens when a traveller dies.

My Granny Lucy's funeral (my dad's mum) was one of the first funerals I ever went to. I was young at the time, but I can still remember it to this day. Back then you were to wear black patching on your clothing to show respect for the deceased. This is a tradition that we've held onto with everyone still expected to wear black when a person dies and for days to come afterwards too.

All of Granny Lucy's family and friends were at the funeral, which was in Southend, Essex, and everyone duly wore their black patching. Her funeral was a perfect example of a traveller funeral; she was brought to the cemetery on a traditional horse and cart, and when the ceremony was over we all went back to the local pub.

One funeral tradition that has mostly died out relates to the deceased's belongings. Back in the fifties it was common for mourners to burn the wagon of the deceased; their home and all of their belongings would be set alight as the community said goodbye to their fellow traveller. My Granny Lucy had her wagon burnt after her death. The majority of travellers have not continued this tradition but I think that's mainly because not many travellers live in wagons nowadays, it's more chalets, houses and trailers.

Generally, funerals today have not changed that much since that first funeral that I experienced. One special funeral tradition that has stood the test of time is for mourners to stay up the night before a funeral. This is done as a mark of commemoration and respect for the person that has died. The men typically stay outside, standing in groups around a fire, retelling stories about the deceased and the good times they'd had together. The women keep busy inside, preparing tea and coffee and providing food for everyone to eat throughout the night. Friends and relatives come from far and wide to pay their respects, and nowadays people tend to hire a marquee to provide shelter for the many visitors. This time is referred to as a 'stay up' and the 'stay up' or 'sitting up' can go on for days before the actual funeral. It's a nice way to begin the funeral process, and one that I'm sure will continue for many years to come.

I remember that back in the 50s my mum had a good friend called Rhoda. They lived in Bungay in Suffolk but they stayed in touch regularly. Sadly, Rhoda's husband, Chitty, died and so Mum stepped up to organise the funeral in Kelvedon in Essex; a funeral that closely followed the respected gypsy traditions.

A much happier time in the traveller community is when we all get together for a traveller wedding. As mentioned previously, there has been a real switch from the way we traditionally celebrated weddings, to the way that we do things today. Nowadays, it is not uncommon for the bride to have ten sometimes more bridesmaids and lots of pageboys too. Today's weddings are extravagant affairs! The food at a travellers' wedding is quite extravagant too, and will always include a good range of meats and seafood, a favourite amongst travellers. It's traditional for the bride's father to pay for all of the wedding costs, which can get very expensive! Similarly it's tradition for the groom's mother and father to pay for the honeymoon.

At the reception a bride and her father will share a special song that they dance to, and a traveller bride will always adhere to the tradition of having something old, something new, something borrowed and something blue.

But of course, before we even get to the wedding stage there are also set traditions concerning the courting process. Amongst travellers, when a boy and girl meet and decide that they like each other, after a short time the boy must go to the girl's father and ask him if he can court the girl; this demonstrates respect for both the father and the girl. There is to be no woodrosing (meaning sleeping) together before marriage, which means all young traveller couples must wait until they are romered (meaning married). Once they have been courting for some time, if they do wish to get married then once again the boy must go back to the girl's father and ask him for her hand in marriage. Respecting these traditions is very important amongst the traveller community.

Chapter 10

The End of an Era

My amazing father Daniel passed away on the 29th June 1983; he died of a heart attack. It was a very upsetting time for us all, especially my mum who took the news very hard; she deteriorated rapidly after my father's death, becoming very unwell.

On the night before my father's funeral, people came from all over the country to gather at his home to 'sit up'. The women, including myself, made the tea for all the guests that turned up… my father was a popular man, which meant a lot of tea was made that day!

On the day of the funeral my father was dressed in his corded trousers, the shirt that he'd cut the collar off of, his brown lace up boots and his scarf. Placed in the coffin with him was his favourite hat, the one that he always wore, as if it were his trademark. My father had always said he wanted to be buried in the clothes he always wore, and it was only right that we respected his wishes.

On the morning of the funeral my father's place filled up very quickly with people coming to honour him. He was a well-respected man and the sheer volume of people that were piling into his home reflected that fact. He had made lots of friends along the way and he came from a very large family, so it wasn't a surprise to see cars parking all the way to the end of the road. When the time came to leave my father's home in Little Totham, he was taken in a black Maria car which drove the long way round to Kelvedon church; along the way it passed Little Braxted, and as we were approaching Kelvedon we drove up a chase known as Shan's Chase, where my family had carried out field work for many years. Finally we came to Kelvedon Church where hundreds of people were waiting for my father's arrival. The wreaths that were made for him were absolutely extraordinary. I couldn't quite comprehend that people had gone to so much effort to make these tributes that really were out of this world. One in particular took centre stage; it was made by a man named Dave Wheat; he'd made a wreath in the shape of a wagon, and it was so impressive that it was actually pictured in the newspaper at the time and is now on show in the Museum of East Anglian Life.

The famous wagon and horse wreath

The press took a real interest in the funeral and the wreaths, mainly because I don't think they had ever seen anything quite like it. It was covered across several pages of the local newspaper; I think they needed that much space to get to grips with the magnitude of it all.

And whilst the wreaths and numbers of mourners were truly eye opening, the actual ceremony was extremely emotional. I walked in with my Mum, Sister Lilly and Brothers Mark, John and Richard, and behind us followed our husbands, wives and all the grandchildren, who in turn were followed by friends. There were so many people in attendance that they couldn't all fit in the church, so people were stood respectfully outside and gathered far down the road. The song 'Rosemary' by Slim Whitman was played for the entrance; it had always been one of my father's favourites, and one that he sang to my mother on many occasions. He loved music, with another of his favourite songs being 'Don't Laugh At Me Cause I'm A Fool' by Norman Wisdom. The mourners all stood respectfully as the beautiful melody of 'The Old Rugged Cross' filled every corner of the building and the packed church paid their respects.

The wagon and horse wreath at the graveside

The burial continued to see a wave of emotions as we all said our goodbyes, then, when it was all over we solemnly headed back to the common land behind my father's home. We had hired a marquee and erected it there, and appointed caterers to feed the hordes of people that wanted to remember his life. Everyone stayed until the early evening and I remember thinking how well my mother had done to get through the highly emotional day with such dignity and grace.

When the dust settled Mum chose to stay at home in their family home; understandably she didn't want to live anywhere else. It was hard for her though, to be without her life partner; she struggled without the great Daniel Buckley by her side. We all did.

The wreath displayed in the Museum of East Anglian Life

After just a few days it became clear just how hard that struggle was for my mother. She wasn't in a good way, she missed my father terribly as we all did, and she started to neglect herself. We did our best to make sure that she was eating well, as she had stopped cooking for herself after Dad passed away. We all mucked in to look after her though; my sister in-law, Silvy, lived right near her and so she would cook and take food over for her, making sure she ate it all before she left too. My brother Richard and sister in-law Lena would take her for a drive out to get her out of the house for a little while, and my brother John, would make sure that Mum was ok at night, and check around to make sure everything was in place. My brother Mark and sister in-law, Una, would go and check on Mum throughout the day to see if there was anything she needed. Whilst my sister Lilly would take Mum to her home so she had a change of scenery. I would take Mum out and bring her to my home to cook for her as well as do the chores; having us all live so nearby made looking after her a lot easier.

Mourners viewing the wreaths

The first year after my father passed away was hard, especially with winter coming up; we all had to make sure things were looked after outside as Dad wouldn't have wanted things to slip just because he wasn't there.

But we all had our own chores to do at our own places, so we all had to muck in and do our bit. None of us wanted to let Mum stay on her own at home, and we were all willing to house her in our own homes, but she insisted she stayed put... she didn't want to be anywhere else apart from home; which I could understand. By the spring things were starting to get a little easier as my dad had been gone nearly a year; we still all missed him very much though. It seemed strange not seeing him out on the common land looking after his horses, or going to work with a truck full of logs to sell. There was a definite void in our lives.

Ford D series carrying the wreaths to the funeral

Looking after Mum kept us busy though, along with looking after our own families and doing our own chores of course. But it was clear that the void in Mum's life was too big to fill. Even after the first year she continued to deteriorate; it was as if she had no reason to exist without her soulmate. She gave up looking after herself, which was painful for the rest of us to witness. She was simply lost without him. From not cooking anymore, to not going out, we soon found that Mum became bedbound... unable or unwilling to even attempt to change her circumstances. She was giving up.

● David Weekes and Danal Buckley's widow Doris by the huge wreath.

A multi-coloured labour of love

Report: EMMA SHARP
Picture: TONY TUNBRIDGE

AN antiques dealer has just completed a most unusual deal — making a massive wreath for the grave of gipsy king Danal Buckley who died in June.

The wreath has been commissioned by the Buckley family who live at Little Totham Plains.

Why has a florist's job fallen to an antiques dealer? Well, before David Weekes started in the antiques trade he was a florist, though that was 32 years ago when he was 18.

And the other reason is that professional florists, according to Mr Weekes,

were not too keen on tackling the huge task as the wreath is eight feet long, three feet wide and five feet tall.

COLOURS

About 2,000 artificial flowers went into making the magnificent wreath which depicts a horse-drawn gypsy caravan.

A total of $200 of flowers have been used in six different varieties and about ten different colours.

Mr Weekes, who runs the antiques shop at the corner of Coggeshall Road and Cressing Road, Braintree, said the job was a real labour of love.

He spent 200 hours and four weeks completing it.

Said Mr Weekes: " I last worked as a florist when I was 18, but the family came to me because they knew me.

" I have thoroughly enjoyed making it and spent every spare minute working on it in the garage."

The wreath is built on a wooden frame and should last up to six months according to Mr Weekes.

" The cost of making it will definitely be four figures," he added.

STALLION

The wreath was taken to the graveside at St Mary's Church, Kelvedon by horse-drawn carriage, with the 50 members of the Buckley family in a procession.

" Horses were my grandfather's life," said grandson John Buckley.

" He must have had 30 or 40 at one time.

" Next year we want to have a stallion made for his grave."

Press coverage of Daniel's funeral

In 1987 my dear mum became very unwell; she never complained though, even when she was at her worst. It was August when we finally lost her, passing away at home, four years after I'd lost my father. It was a terribly difficult time for me and everyone who loved her.

Her funeral was held in late August, with an affair similar to my father's funeral, as we all knew that was what they would have wanted. Once again people came from all over to pay their respects the night before, and to my mother's home the next day before the funeral itself. My mum was dressed in the clothes she loved and wore the most, and people gathered at her home in Little Totham, just as they had done on the day of my father's funeral. A black, Maria car, the same as Dad's funeral car drove Mum from Little Totham through the exact same route as my father, through Little Braxted, Kelvedon and to Kelvedon church where people were waiting, lined up respectfully down the road on the green. Mum was well loved and the huge number of people that were there that day just proved that. Not everyone could fit into the church, and those that couldn't simply waited respectfully outside. After the service my mother was buried with my father; the formidable couple reunited again.

The wake was held at Kelvedon Hall where we booked caterers to prepare food for the many people that stayed for hours and hours just talking and reminiscing about Dolly and Daniel Buckley.

After my mother's death things seemed different for everyone. The emptiness that we'd all felt when my father passed away was now doubled. Things just didn't seem the same as they did before, for any of us.

My daughter, Marisa, arrived into the world three weeks after my mum passed away. She was born at the same hospital I'd had my other children in and she was a welcome distraction from the grief and sense of loss I was feeling about my mum. I'll never understand how it's possible to be overwhelmed by sadness and happiness all at once.

I was in hospital for four days with Marisa, and when I returned home things were a lot easier than when I'd had my other children as by this time there was no field work to be done, although I was still constantly on the go. But the loss and grief I was feeling made things difficult. We all comforted each other though, Josie and Karl helped me a lot, and thankfully my husband, Eddie, was a real rock for me too; I needed their help more than ever as I had a newborn baby to care for and my mind and heart were both heavily burdened with the loss of my parents.

They say time is a great healer, and it's true, after a while I began to accept that my mother and father were no longer around. It wasn't easy and I still miss them to this day; and when things get tough I often think about one of my dad's favourite sayings, "Why Worry?" He was right of course, as he was about most things.

We somehow found the strength to carry on with life. We all stayed put where we were living as we were settled down now, and we continued working hard and raising our family. I regularly visit my parents' grave to take flowers and make sure they are kept clean and tidy. And the memories of them are still very much present in our hearts and minds. Even now we often talk about them, about the good old days and all that they taught us over the years.

Daniel and Dolly Buckley really were one of a kind, and as their proud daughter I couldn't have asked for better parents and role models. I had a happy childhood and they taught me about working hard, the Romany way of life and the importance of family. Their love for their family was immense and they would have loved to have seen how big our family has grown since their passing.

L-R: Mary, Una, Lilly, Sylvie, Lena

If I had to estimate how many people there are in my family now, I would say at least two hundred, and even now as I write this book there are more babies on the way. I know for certain that my parents would be proud of all their children, grandchildren and great grandchildren, who are all living their lives to the fullest and enjoying the Romany way of life, thanks to them.

I truly am proud to be a Romany gypsy, and I wouldn't and couldn't live my life any other way. I am who I am because of the guidance and love shown to me by my parents. The Romany values and traditions that they surrounded me with as I was growing up have stayed with me to this day, and I hope that they will continue to be passed on through the generations to come.

★ ★ ★ ★

I have really enjoyed researching my parents' lives, and reminiscing about my life as I child. It has given me great pleasure to connect with other family members and share stories and tales about times that some of us had forgotten. The photographs that we found during the process of writing this book have conjured up great memories for all of us, and I hope that you have enjoyed reading our story too.